See for Yourself

Smell and Taste

See for Yourself

Smell and Taste

Brenda Walpole
Photographs by Barrie Watts

RSVP
RAINTREE
Steck-Vaughn
PUBLISHERS
The Steck-Vaughn Company

Austin, Texas

Published by Raintree Steck-Vaughn Publishers, an imprint of Steck-Vaughn Company

Editor: Kathy DeVico
Project Manager: Amy Atkinson
Electronic Production: Scott Melcer

All photographs by Barrie Watts except for:
p. 9 Thomas Raupach/Still Pictures; p. 11 Shout Pictures; p. 13 E. A. James/NHPA
p. 15,16 Sally Anne Thompson/Animal Photography; p. 17 T. Kitchin & V. Hurst/
NHPA; p. 21 David Young-Wolff/PhotoEdit; p. 27 National Dairy Council

Library of Congress Cataloging-in-Publication Data
Walpole, Brenda.
    Smell and taste / Brenda Walpole; photographs by Barrie Watts.
        p.   cm. — (See for yourself)
    Includes index.
    Summary: Introduces the concept of smell and taste and suggests activities which reinforce the understanding of these senses.
    ISBN 0-8172-4215-5
    1. Taste — Juvenile literature.   2. Smell — Juvenile literature.   [1. Taste.   2. Smell.   3. Senses and sensation.]
    I. Watts, Barrie, ill.   II. Title.   III. Series.
    QP456.W35   1997
    612.8'6 — dc20   96-6957
                                                      CIP
                                                      AC

Printed and bound in the United States
1 2 3 4 5 6 7 8 9 0 LB 99 98 97 96

Contents

What Smells Can Tell Us

What is your favorite smell?

Our sense of smell tells us a lot about the world around us. Smells remind us of people and places that we know. And the smells of some foods tell us that they are good to eat.

Which smells remind you of the spring? Or of dinnertime? Can you imagine the smell of the freshly cut grass in the big picture?

Every house has its own smell, although the people who live there may not notice it. Make a "smell map" of your home. Draw pictures of things you might smell in the kitchen, in the bathroom, and in your bedroom.

How Our Noses Work

Hold your nose. Can you still smell things?

Your sense of smell comes from a special patch of skin inside your nose. When you breathe in, smells are carried into your nose through your nostrils. When they pass over this special skin, the skin sends messages to the brain about the smells. If you want to smell something more strongly, you can sniff to get extra scent into your nose.

You can get used to smells when you have smelled them for a long time— even smells you don't like. People who work in garbage dumps get so used to the smell that they hardly notice it.

The more scent you breathe in, the stronger something will smell. The girl in this picture is close to the fruit. She can smell it very easily. But what will happen as she moves farther away?

Warning Smells

Smells can tell you that something is bad or dangerous.

The smell of smoke may mean that there is a fire.
The smell of gas may be a sign that there is a gas leak.
If you ever smell gas, you should tell a grown-up right away.

When milk goes sour, it smells terrible. So do fruits when they get moldy.

Look at the pictures below.
Which of these foods
smell awful when
they have spoiled?
Which doesn't smell
too bad, even when
it is no longer fresh?

How Animals and Insects Smell

Many animals have a very good sense of smell. Some animals, such as dogs, have a much better sense of smell than humans. Animals need sensitive noses to find their food.

Pigs have big, moist snouts that can sniff out food that has been buried under the ground. When wild pigs find food, they use their nose like a shovel to help them dig it up.

Some insects do not smell with a nose. For example, moths have very sensitive antennae, which they use to smell their surroundings. They can smell other moths from over a mile away.

Many other insects smell things through antennae, feelers, or different parts of their body. Can you find out how ants or flies smell things?

Sensitive Noses

Dogs can use their sense of smell to help us find things.
Bloodhounds are used as trackers. They are very good
at finding people who have run away or gotten lost.
As they sniff the ground, they pick up the scent that a
person has left behind. They can follow it for many miles.
A bloodhound has long, floppy ears that hang close to the
ground. These ears carry smells right into the dog's nose.

St. Bernard dogs use their keen sense of smell to help find
people who are buried in the snow. They have saved many
people's lives.

Can you find out which of these animals also has a very
good sense of smell? You will find the answer on page 28.

How Animals Use Smell

Dogs can remember people and other animals by their smell. They greet other dogs and their owners by sniffing them carefully.

If you stroke a cat, it may rub its face against your hand. As it does, it rubs a little of its scent onto you. The smell tells the cat that you are a friend.

By rubbing against things, cats mark an area as theirs. This area is called their territory. They may attack other cats that enter their territory.

Some animals use scent to drive their enemies away. Skunks spray a smelly liquid when an enemy comes too near. Just seeing the skunk's black-and-white tail is enough to make some attackers run away.

Flowers and Their Scents

Many flowers are scented or have colorful petals.
The colors and smells attract insects, which then come to feed
on the nectar inside the flowers. As the insects feed, pollen from
the flowers rubs onto them. The insects carry pollen from one
flower to the next. Flowers need pollen to make new seeds.

You can see for yourself how the smells from flowers attract insects.
Choose three different kinds of flowers that are the same color.
You might find them in your school playground or near your home.
Watch the flowers for ten minutes. Then count the number of insects
that visit each one. Which flowers are visited the most? Do they have a strong scent? Why is it important to choose flowers that are the same color?

How Do We Use Scents?

To make our homes smell nice, we use perfumes that smell like flowers and plants. The smells remind us of clean and fresh places, like gardens, woods, or mountains.

Disinfectants, dish detergents, soaps, and air fresheners all have perfumes added to them. They might smell like lemon, pine trees, or jasmine flowers.

Look for all the things in your home that are scented. Which perfumes have been used to give them their smell?

Lavender flowers smell for a long time after they have been picked. You can keep an envelope filled with lavender in your drawer to make your clothes smell fresh.

Look at the objects below. Which ones would also give your clothes a fresh smell? Which one would not?

How Smell and Taste Work Together

When you eat, you taste the food with your tongue.
At the same time, smells from the food go into your nose.
Your senses of smell and taste work together so that you
can decide if you like the flavor of the food.

If your sense of smell isn't working, you can't taste very well.
When you have a cold, your nose can become blocked.
Do your favorite foods taste as good
if you can't smell them?

Try holding your nose and
eating a slice of apple. Then
try again with a piece of
pear. Can you taste them?
Try the same test with
your eyes closed. Do you
know which of the fruits
is the apple, if you can't
see or smell it?

Tongues

Look closely at your tongue in a mirror. Can you see that it has little bumps on it? There are about nine thousand bumps on your tongue, and each one has taste buds on it.

Taste buds give you a sense of taste. You can sense four tastes: sweet, sour, salty, and bitter. Most foods are a mixture of all four tastes.

Some parts of your tongue are more sensitive to certain tastes. You can test your own taste buds. Stick out your tongue. Sprinkle a few grains of salt onto its tip. Can you taste the salt? Rinse your mouth with water. Try a sprinkle of salt in the middle and on the sides of your tongue. Where can you taste the salt best? That is where you have the most salt taste buds.

WARNING:
Never taste anything unless you know it is safe to taste. Ask a grown-up to help you.

24

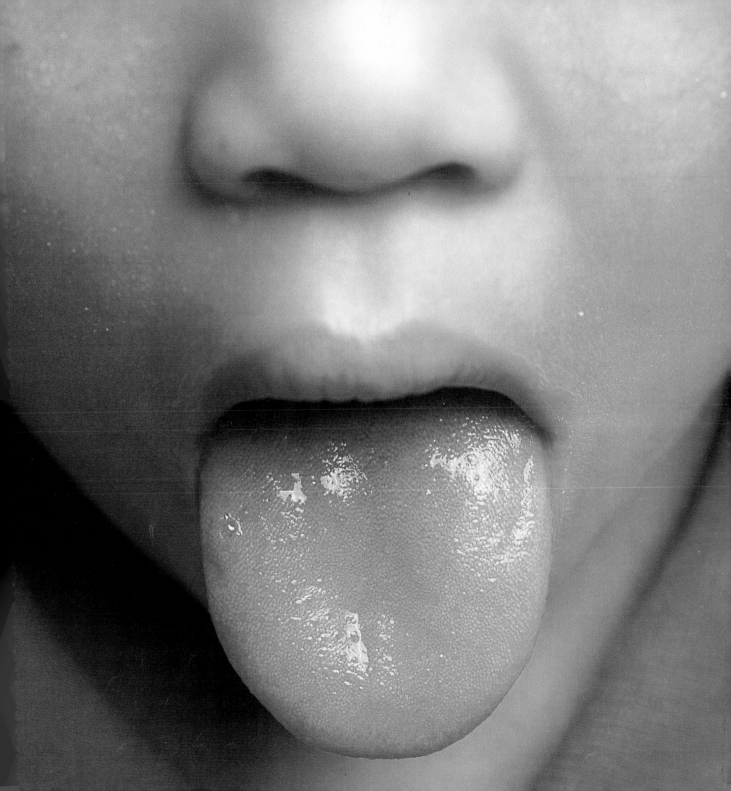

Jobs that Use Smell and Taste

The man in the photograph is a cheese taster.
His nose and tongue are very sensitive.
He can tell when a cheese is ripe and ready to be eaten.

Other people with sensitive noses work as tea or coffee tasters. They check the flavor and smell of each type before it is packaged to be sold.

You can test a friend's sense of smell. Find some fruits and spices that have strong smells. Ask an adult to help you cut up the fruits. Put each one in a clean yogurt container. Cover the containers with black paper, and make holes in the tops. Ask your friend to sniff each container and then guess what is inside.

More Things to Do

1. Not everyone can smell the same things. Freesias are flowers that smell beautiful to some people. Other people can't smell them at all. Test some of your family members to see who can smell freesias. The ability to smell freesias is inherited. You might use the test to trace how this ability has been passed down through your family.

2. Changing the color of food
The way food looks, as well as its smell, helps us decide whether we like it. Take three glasses of water. Color one with orange food coloring, and a second with blue food coloring. (Even though the color changes, the taste of the water will remain the same.) Do not add anything to the third glass. Ask friends to taste each one and say which they like best.

Answer for page 14:
Deer have a very good sense of smell. If the wind is blowing in the right direction, they can smell an enemy that has killed recently at a distance of two miles.
Some birds, such as the kiwi, can detect different smells. However, most birds don't have a very good sense of smell.

Index

This index will help you find some
of the important words in this book.

Notes for Parents and Teachers

These notes will give you some additional information about the senses and suggest some more activities you might like to try with children.

Pages 8–9
Smell receptor cells are located inside the top of the nose. As smell molecules stimulate them, they send messages to the brain. Smell molecules diffuse through the air and decrease in concentration as they move away from their source.

Pages 12–13
Crabs and flies have sensory hairs on their feet that sample chemicals. These hairs allow them to taste food as they walk over it. Ants have smell receptors on their legs.

Many aquatic vertebrates have a good sense of smell. A shark has receptors in its nose that respond particularly well to the scent of blood molecules that have dissolved in water. Whales and porpoises, however, have no receptors and so no sense of smell.

Pages 14–17
A bloodhound is estimated to have thirty times the number of smell receptors of a person. This gives the bloodhound a sense of smell that is about one million times more efficient than our own.

Many animals, such as deer and dogs, mark their territories with scents. You could ask the children to imagine how they would mark an area—perhaps their bedroom or their house—as their territory. What scent would they choose if they wanted to scare off enemies?

Pages 18–19
By choosing flowers that are the same color, the children will ensure that smell alone is attracting the insects to the flowers.

Some flowers, such as roses, lavender, and marigolds, smell strongest during the day. Insects that visit them fly around in the daytime. Honeysuckle smells strongest in the evening. It is visited by moths that come out when it's nearly dark. The children could find out about other flowers that smell strongly at night, and investigate why this might be so.

Pages 22–25
Our senses of taste and smell work together. Vapor from the food being eaten passes through the back of the mouth to the receptors in the nose.

The majority of the taste receptors are at the tip and around the edges of the tongue. Sweet and salty tastes are registered by buds at and just behind the tip of the tongue. Taste buds responding to sour tastes are located at the sides. Bitter taste buds are at the back of the mouth.

30